THE SENSES

The Sense of Sight

by Mari Schuh

Consultant:
Eric H. Chudler, Ph.D.
Director, Neuroscience for Kids
University of Washington
Seattle, Wash.

BLASTOFF!
4
READERS

Note to Librarians, Teachers, and Parents:

Blastoff! Readers are carefully developed by literacy experts and combine standards-based content with developmentally-appropriate text.

Level 1 provides the most support through repetition of high-frequency words, light text, predictable sentence patterns, and strong visual support.

Level 2 offers early readers a bit more challenge through varied simple sentences, increased text load, and less repetition of high frequency words.

Level 3 advances early-fluent readers toward fluency through increased text and concept load, less reliance on visuals, longer sentences, and more literary language.

Level 4 builds reading stamina by providing more text per page, increased use of punctuation, greater variation in sentence patterns, and increasingly challenging vocabulary.

Level 5 encourages children to move from "learning to read" to "reading to learn" by providing even more text, varied writing styles, and less familiar topics.

Whichever book is right for your reader, Blastoff! Readers are the perfect books to build confidence and encourage a love of reading that will last a lifetime!

This edition first published in 2008 by Bellwether Media.

No part of this publication may be reproduced in whole or in part without written permission of the publisher. For information regarding permission, write to Bellwether Media Inc., Attention: Permissions Department, Post Office Box 1C, Minnetonka, MN 55345-9998.

Library of Congress Cataloging-in-Publication Data
Schuh, Mari C., 1975–
  The sense of sight / by Mari Schuh.
    p. cm. – (Blastoff! readers: the senses)
Summary: "Introductory text explains the function and experience of the sense of sight. Intended for grades two through five"–Provided by publisher.
  Includes bibliographical references and index.
  ISBN-13: 978-1-60014-071-6 (hardcover : alk. paper)
  ISBN-10: 1-60014-071-8 (hardcover : alk. paper)
  1. Vision–Juvenile literature. I. Title.

  QP475.7.S38 2008
  612.8'4–dc22

                                   2007022854

Contents

Your Sense of Sight

Look around. What do you see? You're using your sense of sight. Your other senses are hearing, touch, taste, and smell.

Your sense of sight lets
you see close up and
far away. You can see
all the colors of the
rainbow. You can see
different shapes and
sizes. How does your
sense of sight work?
It starts with light.
Light bounces off
of objects and
into your eyes.

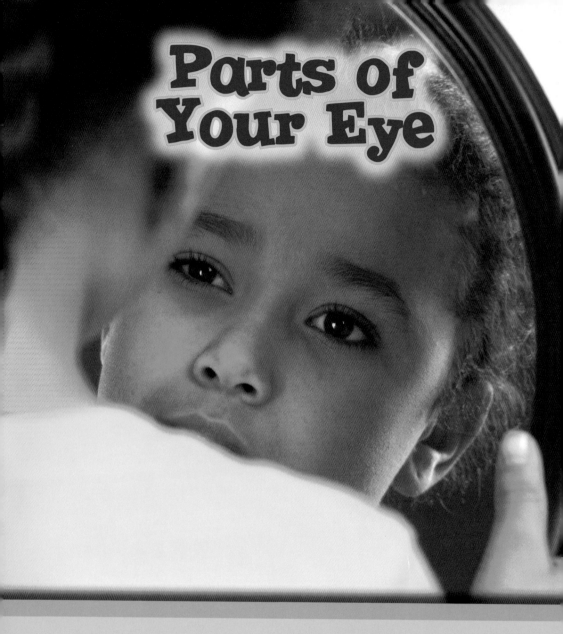

Parts of Your Eye

Look in a mirror. Take a close look at your eyes. Do you see your **pupils**?

Your pupils are the small black circles in the middle of your eyes. The circles are really holes. The holes let in light.

Your pupils change size. They get bigger when you are somewhere with low light. Bigger pupils let in more of the surrounding light so you can see better. The size of a pupil depends on the **iris**. The iris is the colored part of your eye. It has many small muscles. They move to change the size of your pupil.

! fun fact

Eyelashes help protect your eyes. Each of your eyes has about 200 eyelashes. An eyelash lasts for a few months. Then it falls out and a new eyelash takes its place.

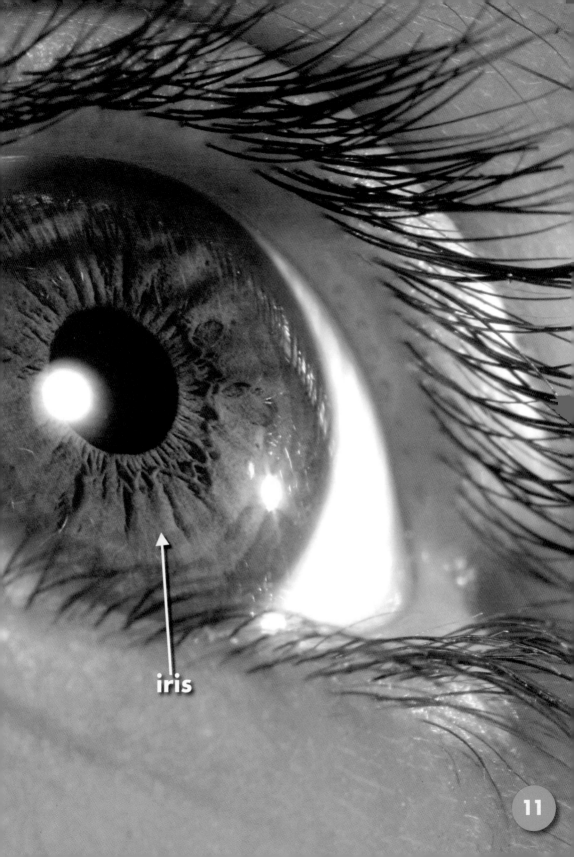

iris

How You See

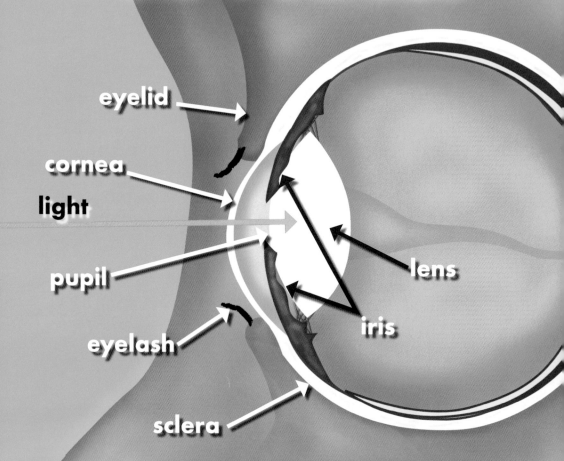

eyelid

cornea

light

pupil

eyelash

sclera

lens

iris

Light passes through many parts of your eye. It first travels through a clear covering called the **cornea**.

Then light goes through your pupil and into the **lens**. The lens **focuses** the light. It makes things you see sharp and clear. It helps you see objects that are close up or far away.

! fun fact
Most people blink about 12 times a minute. That's about 10,000 to 12,000 blinks every day!

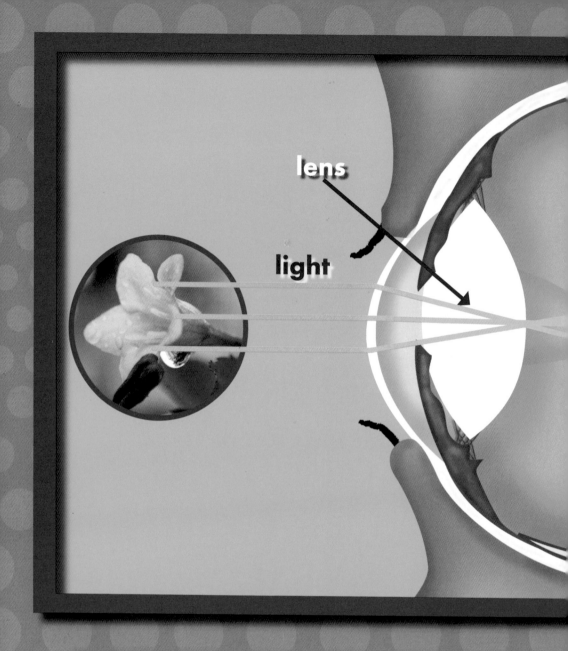

lens

light

The focused light travels to the **retina** at the back of your eye. The retina turns the light into messages.

14

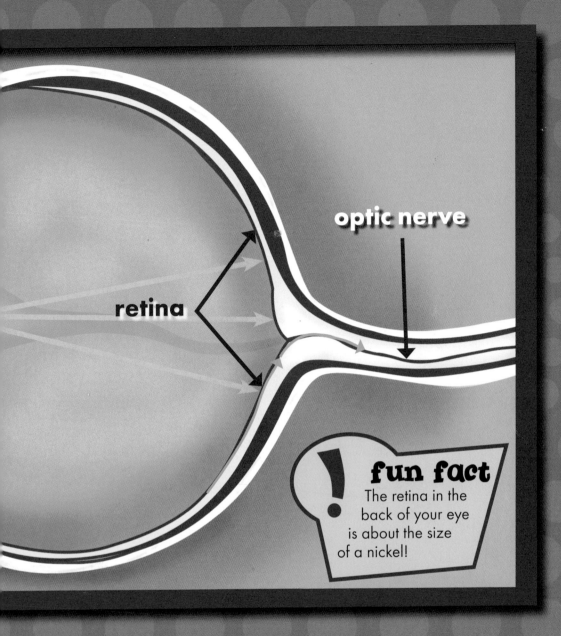

optic nerve

retina

The **optic nerve** behind your eyeball sends the messages to your brain. Your brain then makes a picture of what you see.

Some people's lenses have trouble focusing light. They either have trouble seeing objects up close or far away. Glasses and **contact lenses** can correct focusing problems. They can help these people see much better.

Some people are color-blind. They find it hard to tell one color from another. Someone who is color-blind might mistake red for green.

Animals and Sight

Many animals can see better than people. Eagles can spot rabbits, fish, and other prey from a mile away!

Eagles can dive toward the earth at 100 miles (161 kilometers) per hour. They can keep their prey in focus the entire time.

! fun fact

Camels have eyelashes that are 4 inches (10 centimeters) long. Long eyelashes protect their eyes in sandstorms.

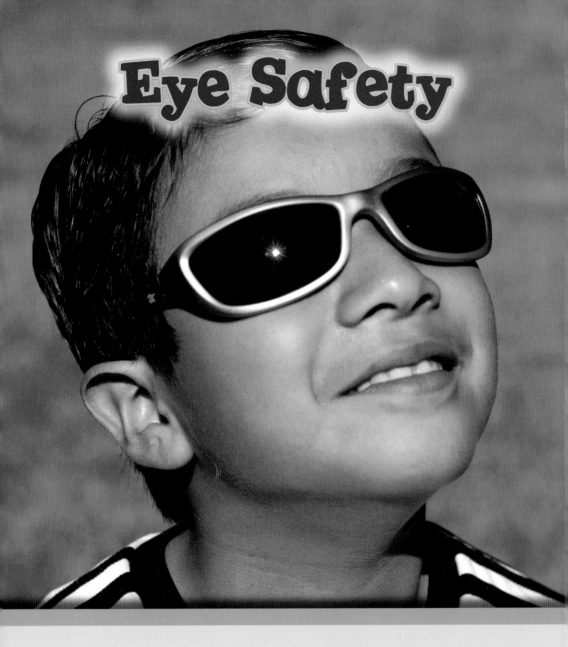

Eye Safety

Taking care of your eyes is important. Never look directly at the sun. Wear sunglasses on sunny days. Reading by dim light can make your eyes tired. Be sure to read where there is enough light.

Your sense of sight lets you see the world around you. Imagine your life without your sense of sight. How would it be different?

Glossary

contact lenses—thin plastic or glass lens fitted over the eye to correct a person's sight

cornea—the clear outer layer of the eye; the cornea is thin but strong.

focus—to make what you see sharp and clear

iris—the round, colored part of the eye around the pupil; the iris has muscles that control the size of the pupil.

lens—the part of the eye that focuses light and sends it to the retina; the lens is right behind the iris.

optic nerve—a long, thin body part behind each eyeball; optic nerves send messages to the brain.

pupil—the round, black part of the eye that lets light pass through it; the pupil is really a small hole.

retina—the thin lining on the back of the eye; the retina sends messages to the optic nerve.

sclera—the white material covering the entire eyeball except for the cornea

To Learn More

AT THE LIBRARY
Curry, Don L. *Take Care of Your Eyes*. New York: Children's Press, 2005.

Douglas, Lloyd G. *My Eyes*. New York: Children's Press, 2004.

Gray, Susan Heinrichs. *The Eyes*. Chanhassen, Minn.: Child's World, 2006.

Mackill, Mary. *Seeing*. Chicago, Ill.: Heinemann, 2006.

Woodward, Kay. *Sight*. Milwaukee, Wisc.: Gareth Stevens, 2006.

ON THE WEB
Learning more about sight is as easy as 1, 2, 3.

1. Go to www.factsurfer.com

2. Enter "sight" into search box.

3. Click the "Surf" button and you will see a list of related web sites.

With factsurfer.com, finding more information is just a click away.

Index

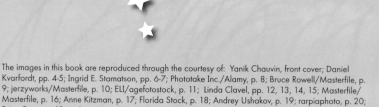

The images in this book are reproduced through the courtesy of: Yanik Chauvin, front cover; Daniel Kvarfordt, pp. 4-5; Ingrid E. Stamatson, pp. 6-7; Phototake Inc./Alamy, p. 8; Bruce Rowell/Masterfile, p. 9; jerzyworks/Masterfile, p. 10; ELI/agefotostock, p. 11; Linda Clavel, pp. 12, 13, 14, 15; Masterfile/Masterfile, p. 16; Anne Kitzman, p. 17; Florida Stock, p. 18; Andrey Ushakov, p. 19; rarpiaphoto, p. 20; Brian Summers/Getty Images, p. 21.